HEALING BELONGS TO US

By Kenneth E. Hagin

Thirteenth Printing 1983

ISBN 0-89276-016-8

In the U.S. write:
Kenneth Hagin Ministries
P.O. Box 51026
Tulsa, Oklahoma 74150

In Canada write:
Kenneth Hagin Ministries
P.O. Box 335
Islington (Toronto), Ontario
Canada, M9A 4X3

Copyright © 1969 RHEMA Bible Church
AKA Kenneth Hagin Ministries, Inc.
All Rights Reserved
Printed in USA

CONTENTS

CHAPTER I

When Healing Doesn't Come

"I have prayed and prayed. I have been in healing meetings all over the country and have been prayed for many times, but still I am not healed. Can you help me?"

This plaintive appeal has been heard many times by healing ministers everywhere. They pray for these sick persons, but usually they go away as they came—unhealed. Why is it that some are healed instantly while others trudge from place to place seeking healing, only to be disappointed time after time? Why is it that some who are pillars in the church often suffer for years with their afflictions while others who are less devout receive a sudden miracle from God? Is God a respecter of persons? Or have we failed in our approach to healing, lacking a complete understanding of what God's Word teaches on the subject? In this book we will look to the scriptures for the answers.

Much emphasis has been placed on the practice of laying on of hands, anointing with oil, praying for the sick. But there is more to healing than just anointing with oil, just as there is more to salvation than just prayer. The anointing oil, the minister's prayer, the laying on of hands—these are just methods or points of contact. They will not heal you. These are just avenues through which we can release our faith in God's Word. But if we do not know what God's Word says, we cannot release our faith in God's Word. Then we just release our faith in laying

3

on of hands or anointing with oil, and are disappointed when these won't work.

Much emphasis has also been placed on the gifts of healings which are among the gifts of the Spirit mentioned in I Corinthians 12:8-10. *"For to one is given by the Spirit the word of wisdom; to another the word of knowledge by the same Spirit; To another faith by the same Spirit; to another* **the gifts of healings** *by the same Spirit; to another the working of miracles; to another prophecy; to another discerning of spirits; to another divers kinds of tongues; to another the interpretation of tongues."*

There will be manifestations of these supernatural gifts where people preach them, teach them, believe in them, and yield to the Spirit of God. But these gifts are not always in operation. Many times new Christians have been healed by such special manifestations. Then the next time they are sick, instead of believing God's Word, they expect to be healed again in the same way, and they are disappointed when they are not.

I have found in my ministry of many years that usually these supernatural manifestations of healing are seen either among denominational people who have not heard divine healing taught, or sinners. I have seldom— if ever—seen them work for Full Gospel people. The believer should be healed by releasing his faith in the Word of God. Gifts of healings and supernatural manifestations are given primarily to advertise the gospel and to gain the attention of those outside the church.

In one of my meetings I pointed to a fellow and said, "Sir, you are unsaved, but the Spirit of God shows me that you have a double hernia. If you will come here right this moment, I will lay my hands on you and it will disappear instantly." He did, and it did. At the altar call that night he responded to the invitation and was saved. Two nights later I laid hands on him and he was filled with the Holy Ghost.

We need to distinguish the difference between heal-

4

ings obtained through supernatural gifts or manifestations, and those obtained by exercising faith in God's Word alone.

It must be understood, too, that the individual does not operate these supernatural gifts; they are manifested through him. I can't make them work any time I want. I could say something, but it wouldn't work. I can only stay open for the manifestation of the Spirit of God as the Spirit wills.

Many of us have been taught that the only reason Jesus healed was to prove His deity. If that be the case, He didn't ever prove His deity in the city of Nazareth, for He never did the works there that He had done elsewhere.

"And he (Jesus) *could there* (Nazareth) *do no mighty work, save that he laid his hands upon a few sick folk, and healed them"* (Mark 6:5). Notice that Mark didn't say that He wouldn't do any mighty work there; he said Jesus *couldn't.*

The Amplified New Testament says, "He laid His hands on a few sickly people." In other words, they were just sickly—nothing like blindness or deafness, no crippled, or palsied. W. E. Vine's **Expository Dictionary of New Testament Words** also brings out the fact that the Greek reads, "He laid His hands on a few folk with minor ailments and healed them."

Jesus did not heal people merely to prove His deity. He was not ministering as the Son of God. He was ministering as a prophet of God, anointed with the Spirit. He says in Luke 4:24 *"Verily I say unto you, No prophet is accepted in his own country."* He called Himself a prophet.

In Matthew 13:58 we learn why Jesus could not heal on some occasions. *"And he did not many mighty works there because of their unbelief."* Their unbelief hindered Him.

Also in the fourth chapter of Luke, Jesus said that

5

when there was a great famine through the land during Elijah's time, there were many widows in Israel, *"But unto none of them was Elias sent, save unto Sarepta, a city of Sidon, unto a woman that was a widow"* (Verse 26). Even though Elijah had God's power in his life, he could not make it work for everybody. But because he was sent to this particular widow's house, there was a continuous miracle. The meal barrel never became empty—they just kept dipping meal out of it—and the cruse of oil never ceased to flow.

Jesus went on to say, *"And many lepers were in Israel in the time of Eliseus the prophet; and none of them was cleansed, saving Naaman the Syrian"* (Verse 27). Naaman traveled many miles to reach Samaria where he had heard a prophet could rid him of his leprosy. Yet there were many lepers in Israel at this time and Elisha didn't cure any of them.

Elisha had a double portion of the anointing of the Spirit of God upon him to minister, and the Bible records that he did twice as many miracles as Elijah, his predecessor. There were lepers in Israel, but not one of them was healed. Yet to Naaman, a Syrian, he said, *"Go and wash in Jordan seven times, and thy flesh shall come again to thee, and thou shalt be clean"* (II Kings 5:10).

Why didn't the lepers in Israel go to Elisha and get healed too? The answer lies in the Israelites' covenant of healing with God. In that covenant the Lord said, *"I am the Lord that healeth thee."* In Exodus 23:25-26 He said, *"...I will take sickness away from the midst of thee...the number of thy days I will fulfil."* Then again in Deuteronomy 7:15, *"And the Lord will take away from thee all sickness...."* You see, they didn't really need any prophet to heal them. They needed to believe the covenant that God had established with them. Naaman, who wasn't even under that covenant, believed and was cleansed.

After Naaman was healed, he came back to Elisha's house and offered him much gold and silver, and many changes of raiment because he was so thrilled that he was healed. The prophet wouldn't take any of this because he knew Naaman was trying to pay for his healing. You can't pay for your healing.

Elisha's servant, Gehazi, had a covetous heart and hated to see all that silver and gold and changes of raiment get away. He ran to Naaman and told him a lie: *"My master hath sent me, saying, Behold even now there be come to me from Mount Ephraim two young men of the sons of the prophets: give them, I pray thee, a talent of silver, and two changes of garments"* (II Kings 5:22). Naaman was so thrilled to be healed of his leprosy he gave him twice as much as he asked for. Then Gehazi took the clothing, the gold and silver, and hid it because he was getting it for his own use.

When Gehazi returned, Elisha said, *"...Whence comest thou, Gehazi? And he said, Thy servant went no whither. And he said unto him, Went not mine heart with thee, when the man turned again from his chariot to meet thee?..."* (Verses 25, 26). In his spirit Elisha had seen Gehazi join Naaman's chariot. He knew exactly what he had done. Elisha wasn't aware of every lie that had been told in the land that day. He didn't know everyone who had been stealing. Naturally there were many others besides Gehazi who were guilty of lying and stealing, but Elisha just had a supernatural manifestation concerning this one.

Some think that if someone is a prophet, he is a seer and knows everything. However, the gifts of the Spirit are not in operation all the time, but only as the Spirit wills. Gehazi knew this too, for although he knew Elisha to be a man of God who had supernatural manifestations in his life, Gehazi knew that the word of knowledge operated only occasionally. Otherwise, he wouldn't have been foolish enough to try to lie to Elisha—he would have known that he couldn't get by with it.

We should stay open for manifestations of the Spirit of God, but we do not have to wait on a supernatural manifestation to be delivered from anything that is wrong with us. The gifts of healings have been manifested in my ministry many times, but that does not mean I can make it work for everybody, any more than Elisha could make it work for everybody. I can't push some button or pull some lever and it will start working. It operates as the Spirit wills, for He is doing it, not I.

Healing belongs to us. It isn't just a matter of prayer. It isn't just a matter of some spiritual gift in operation. Healing belongs to us because it has been provided for us by the Lord Jesus Christ.

I endeavor to help sick people understand this. I want to help them get healed one way or another—either by supernatural manifestations of the Spirit of God in my ministry or by getting God's Word into them so that faith will rise in their own hearts. Then when I do lay hands on them and pray, through our mutual faith they will receive their healing.

When I was holding a tent meeting in Oklahoma in August, 1951, our day services were held in a church in the city and night services were held under a tent in the city park. We laid hands on the sick each night after I had preached, primarily on faith, expecting people to release their faith in God's Word. This laying on of hands was to be a point of contact where they would release their faith, and by their faith and my faith helping them all I could, they would receive their healing.

Also, there were some special manifestations occasionally. One such manifestation occurred the night a mother came for prayer with her 4-year-old boy in her arms. As she carried the child, his little legs dangled from her arms. She told me that he'd had polio when he was 18 months old, and had never walked another step. Although his legs were crippled, the rest of his body had developed normally. As I prayed for him, God wonderfully came down in our midst in a supernatural manifestation of His power, and that little boy started

8

running up and down the platform from one end to the other. A few years ago when my wife and I were holding meetings in Oregon, a man introduced himself to us as that boy's uncle and said, "I thought you would be interested to know that we have just been on vacation down in Oklahoma. My nephew is now 17 years old and is on the first string football team in high school."

We are thankful for God's power. I didn't heal the boy. God did. If I could do it, I would heal every polio victim. I have ministered to a number of them. I have pushed the same button and pulled the same lever, but nothing happened. I wish I could make it work for every one of them, just as Elisha no doubt wished he could have helped every widow in Israel and cleansed every leper. Supernatural manifestations can come only as the Spirit wills, not as Elisha willed, not as I will.

While I was preaching a meeting in Texas, a Pentecostal lady brought her little girl for prayer. This child, who was between 8 and 9 years old, had also been stricken with polio. Her left leg dangled from the hip. A brace was on her foot, but when her mother took the brace off, the child couldn't walk. The limb was wasted away.

This time I felt no supernatural manifestation. This was a matter that I had preached God's Word to her and she believed. I laid hands on the child, prayed—and there was no manifestation. She took the child home, apparently in the same condition.

At home that night the mother took the child's braces off to give her a bath before putting her to bed. The foot still turned. The leg still hung out from the hip. Apparently there was no change. She put her in the tub, then got on her knees and started to bathe her.

"I began to cry and say, 'Lord, I am sorry. I wanted my baby to be healed,' " the mother said. "Then I remembered what Brother Hagin had said and my faith quickened. I believed the Word of God. I believed that healing virtue flowed into her then. It was just a matter of believing God's Word. Suddenly I heard something like dry sticks popping. I looked down and that leg straightened out right in front of my eyes." Both legs became the same size and she could walk normally.

This miracle came as a result of preaching and teaching the Word of God, and of a faithful mother's believing and acting upon God's Word.

I believe in supernatural manifestations. We have them. We expect them. We should expect them. But in the meantime we must preach God's Word, and believers should continue to feed on God's Word concerning divine healing to keep their faith strong. Healing belongs to us.

CHAPTER II

Our Twofold Redemption

"He is despised and rejected of men; a man of sorrows, and acquainted with grief: and we hid as it were our faces from him; he was despised, and we esteemed him not. Surely he hath borne our griefs, and carried our sorrows: yet we did esteem him stricken, smitten of God, and afflicted. But he was wounded for our transgressions, he was bruised for our iniquities: the chastisement of our peace was upon him: and with his stripes we are healed" (Isaiah 53:3-5).

The 53rd chapter of Isaiah holds the key to our redemption, spiritual and physical. The fourth verse reads in the Hebrew. "Surely he hath borne our sicknesses, and carried our pains." In the tenth verse the King James reads, "Yet it pleased the Lord to bruise him; he hath put him to *grief...*" Again that is the word for "sick." The Hebrew literally says, "He hath made him sick."

Matthew 8:17 says, *"That it might be fulfilled which was spoken by Esaias* (Isaiah) *the prophet, saying, Himself took our infirmities, and bare our sicknesses."* Matthew is quoting Isaiah 53:4. Therefore, the correct translation is "Surely he hath borne our sicknesses, and carried our pains," for as Matthew said, "Himself took our infirmities, and bare our sicknesses."

Dr. Robert Young, an able Hebrew scholar and author of **Young's Analytical Concordance**, translated this passage in his **Literal Translation of the Bible** thus: *"He*

11

is despised and left of men, A man of pains, and acquainted with sickness, And as one hiding the face from us, He is despised, and we esteemed him not. Surely our sicknesses he hath borne, And our pains—he hath carried them, And we—we have esteemed him plagued, Smitten of God, and afflicted. And he is pierced for our transgressions, Bruised for our iniquities, The chastisement of our peace is upon him—And by his bruise there is healing to us. All of us like sheep have wandered, Each to his own way we have turned, And Jehovah hath caused to meet on him, The punishment of us all...And Jehovah hath delighted to bruise him, He hath made him sick...With transgressors he was numbered, And he the sin of many hath borne, And for transgressors he intercedeth" (Isaiah 53:3-6, 10, 12).

Dr. Isaac Leeser in his translation of **The Twenty-Four Books of the Old Testament,** translated the Hebrew, *"...he was despised and shunned by men: a man of pains, and acquainted with disease:...but only our diseases did he bare himself, and our pains he carried...and through his bruises was healing granted us...But the Lord was pleased to crush him through disease"*(Isaiah 53:4-5, 10).

Rotherham's translation reads, "He hath laid on him sickness."

Every church believes the portion of scripture in Isaiah 53:6 "...the Lord hath laid on him the iniquity of us all." Why not believe the rest of the chapter too? It goes on to say that "he hath borne our sicknesses, and carried our pains" as well.

If I can believe that God laid my iniquities on Jesus, and because He laid my iniquities on Him there is salvation for me, then I can also believe what this chapter tells me that He also laid my sickness and disease on Jesus. I can believe for my healing.

During one of my meetings a woman brought her daughter for prayer. She was facing major surgery. The Spirit of God revealed to me that this daughter did not believe in divine healing, and that she really didn't want to be prayed for. She had never had any teaching on the subject of divine healing. Her mother had just forced her to come for prayer because her mother was financing her operation. A specialist was coming from Chicago to Oklahoma to perform the operation, and it was going to cost about $6,000.

Folks are not always ready to be prayed for. When you go ahead and pray for them, many times you push them further from God. We should give people an opportunity to hear the Word of God taught before we pray for them. Then they, in faith, can receive the impartation of God's power.

After the mother (who did all the talking) finished telling me all about the girl's forthcoming operation, I said, "Let's sit down and talk a little bit about what the Bible says concerning healing."

"Oh, I'm in a hurry," the mother replied. "I want to get her back home so I can get back here for the night service. I have to drive 240 miles to do that."

I said, "If you are in that big a hurry, you will just have to take her back home without being prayed for. I am not going to pray under the circumstances."

Reluctantly, the mother agreed, saying, "We can only stay ten minutes." Every time I would ask the daughter a question, the mother would answer it. Then she said, "Hurry up and pray for her."

Finally, I asked the daughter point blank, "Do you believe in divine healing?"

She said, "Well, to be honest with you, I don't."

I said, "I knew that the minute you walked in the door, just as if you had told me. That's the reason I wouldn't pray for you. I knew you didn't believe."

Could you pray with someone who is lost, and get them saved without their believing in salvation or in Jesus? You could pray from here to yonder and never get them saved. Could you pray with someone to receive the baptism of the Holy Ghost without their believing in it? Certainly not. Then how are you going to pray for someone and get them healed when they don't even believe in healing?

Someone might say, "God will just heal some of those people to prove it is so." Why doesn't He just save some of them to prove it is so then? Why doesn't He just fill some of them with the Holy Ghost just to prove the baptism of the Holy Ghost is real? God doesn't work that way.

God works on the principle of faith. He gives you His Word so you can have faith. Then He expects you to come according to the Word and believe it. Then He honors that Word. When you don't believe it, when you don't act on it, when you don't honor it, then He doesn't have anything to honor in your life.

The daughter said, "I am going to be honest with you. I just came here because Mama wanted me to come. We are borrowing $6,000 from her, and when you are borrowing money from folks, you just can't say no. I thought I would humor her and come along, even though I wouldn't get anything anyhow."

You won't get something from God just by humoring someone else. You can't ride Mama's coattail into heaven. And you can't ride Mama's coattail into divine healing either.

Then I asked her, "If the Bible said that God laid on Jesus your sickness and your disease, would healing be for you?"

"It certainly would," she said.

I said, "Well, there's a Bible lying right there on that table. Reach over and get it and open it to Matthew 8:17. She opened it and read, 'That it might be fulfilled which was spoken by Esaias the prophet, saying, Himself took our infirmities, and bare our sicknesses.' "

Then I said, "Notice the marginal reference says Isaiah 53:4. Matthew was quoting Isaiah."

She turned to Isaiah 53:4 and read it. As she looked down at the Bible for a minute, I just let that soak in a little bit. She didn't say anything. I didn't push it. Her head was bowed over the Bible. When she looked up, tears glistened in her eyes.

She said, "Brother Hagin, please lay your hands on my head and pray. I will be healed. We won't have to borrow that money from Mama. I won't have to have the operation. Yes, healing belongs to me."

Then she added, "I am sure my pastor doesn't know that, for I believe he is honest and would preach it if he knew it."

"I am sure he would, too," I answered and then laid my hands on her and prayed. She was marvelously healed and didn't have to have an operation.

This didn't come about through any supernatural manifestation. I didn't have any special leading or any special anointing at this time. I simply acted in faith on the Word. God's Word works.

The following year I was preaching at the Full Gospel church in her town. One night someone rolled a fellow into the meeting in a wheel chair. After we laid hands on him and prayed, he got out of that wheel chair and walked. I sat in the wheel chair then, and he jubilantly pushed me up and down an aisle in the church auditorium.

The next night the pastor introduced me to a very distinguished looking gentleman seated on the platform. He was the pastor of the church where the woman's daughter attended.

The pastor told me, "The man in the wheel chair who was here last night and was healed is a member of my church. We built a ramp especially for that fellow so he could come to church, and he never missed a service. This morning I drove downtown, pulled in to the curb to park, and saw him walking down the street. I nearly fainted! For years he has been around these streets in his wheel chair. I jumped out of my car and ran to him to find out what had happened. He said, 'I was at the Full

15

Gospel church last night and there was a preacher there praying for the sick. God healed me.'

"I came over here tonight to express my appreciation to this pastor and church, and to you for holding fast the truth that I hadn't seen. I want to thank you all for this man's healing, and for the knowledge that it is God's work."

After my sermon that night on *Salvation and Healing: The Double Cure,* he asked me, "Would you loan me your sermon notes? I want to preach that same sermon next Sunday morning because my church wants to know what happened. After I have preached it, I am going to ask everyone who is sick to come forward, just like you did, and I will lay my hands on them in the name of Jesus."

All this came about as a result of this one woman's hearing and accepting the fact that healing belonged to her. And healing belongs to you, too. "Surely he hath borne our sicknesses, and carried our pains...." God laid on Jesus our sicknesses and pains and He bore them. That means that the pains and afflictions you may be suffering were laid on Jesus. He actually bore them just as He bore your sins. "He was wounded for our transgressions, he was bruised for our iniquities: the chastisement of our peace was upon him; and with his stripes we are healed."

We believe that God laid our sins on Jesus, and therefore we don't have to bear them. This chapter also says that He laid our sickness on Jesus. You can say, "He laid my sickness on Jesus and made Him sick with my disease." The Word declares that. "He hath made him to be sin, who knew no sin; that we might be made the righteousness of God in him." Not only did He make Him who knew no sin to be sin, but He made Him who knew no sickness to be sickness. He made Him sick with your diseases that you might be perfectly well in Christ.

The scriptures in the 53rd chapter of Isaiah and the 8th chapter of Matthew deal with the disease problem that faces the world today. If they don't, then how can

16

we preach salvation from the 53rd chapter of Isaiah? What right would we have to say that part of it belongs to us and the other part doesn't? But Christ has provided deliverance from sin and sickness for us when He purchased our twofold redemption at Calvary.

CHAPTER III

The Laying on of Hands

God has provided some means to assist our faith to help us receive divine healing. One of the most prominent methods is the laying on of hands. *"...They shall lay hands on the sick, and they shall recover"* (Mark 16:18). Of course, laying on of hands won't heal you. If it would, then there would have been no need for God to lay our sicknesses and diseases on Jesus. He could just have told us to lay hands on one another for healing. The laying on of hands merely helps you to release your faith in the Word of God.

Laying on of hands is one of the fundamental principles of the doctrine of Christ. In Hebrews 6:1-2, it says, *"Therefore leaving the principles of the doctrine of Christ, let us go on unto perfection; not laying again the foundation of repentance from dead works, and of faith toward God. Of the doctrine of baptisms, and of laying on of hands, and of resurrection of the dead, and of eternal judgment."*

There is more to laying on of hands than just for healing. The early New Testament church laid hands on men who were ordained unto the ministry. They laid hands on the seven deacons appointed to serve tables. They also laid hands on believers to be filled with the Holy Ghost. *"Then laid they* (Peter and John) *their hands on them* (the Samaritans), *and they received the Holy Ghost"* (Acts 8:17).

Paul wrote a letter which was to be circulated and read to the churches in Galatia. In it he said, *"He therefore that ministereth to you the Spirit, and worketh miracles among you,*

doeth he it by the works of the law, or by the hearing of faith?"
(Galatians 3:5). Of course, the answer was, "By the hearing of faith." He said that the miracles which were wrought among them, and the Holy Spirit that was ministered was done by the hearing of faith.

The reason we are less successful in a lot of our laying on of hands is because we make a practice of it without the preaching and teaching of God's Word. Too many times in our churches the laying on of hands becomes simply a form, a ritual, an empty formality. We come, hands are laid upon us, but nothing happens.

We seem to have the idea that Jesus went around laying hands on everyone He met, but He didn't.

If we have carelessly read the Bible, we probably think that He healed everyone who was sick everywhere, and that whoever was in reach of Him anywhere automatically received healing. This couldn't be true, however, for when Peter and John went through the gate called Beautiful, just a few days after Jesus had ascended, a man who had been crippled from birth lay there begging alms. The Bible says he was carried there every day. It hadn't been too many days since Jesus had been through that same gate.

If He always healed everyone in Jerusalem and around about, then where did those sick people come from who were brought into the streets that Peter's shadow might fall upon them? (Acts 5:15-16.)

One time Jesus walked up to the pool of Bethesda, and there were five porches, or sheds, around that pool just full of sick people. (An angel came down from heaven every so often and troubled the water, and the first one into the water got healed.) Jesus said to one man, *"...wilt thou be made whole? The impotent man answered him, Sir, I have no man, when the water is troubled, to put me into the pool: but while I am coming, another steppeth down before me. Jesus saith unto him, Rise, take up thy bed, and walk. And immediately the man was made whole, and took up his bed, and*

19

walked...." (John 5:6-9).

Although many sick people were crowded around that pool, if anyone else got healed, I don't know it. I am well satisfied if they had, the Bible would have said so.

We have made it a practice in Full Gospel circles to line people up and lay hands on them and pray for them. Some have gotten healed and some haven't. Some people have been through every healing line in America. I have told many of these people who are chronic seekers for healing and the baptism of the Holy Ghost to attend the day Bible classes. "Don't come back anymore for me to lay hands on you, because every time you come you are getting further away from it. Come here with your Bible, and listen to the Word of God taught. And when faith comes, I will know it."

"And there sat a certain man at Lystra, impotent in his feet, being a cripple from his mother's womb, who never had walked: The same heard Paul speak: who stedfastly beholding him, and perceiving that he had faith to be healed, Said with a loud voice, Stand upright on thy feet. And he leaped and walked"(Acts 14:8-10).

When John Alexander Dowie was having considerable success in his ministry of praying for the sick in Australia before the turn of the century, American newspapers published accounts of some of the healings which had taken place. Therefore, when word got out he was coming to San Francisco and would be staying in a certain hotel, sick people came from all over the United States to be prayed for.

Upon his arrival at the hotel, the manager said to him, "You have to do something. Sick people are lined up for two blocks in every direction from this hotel wanting you to pray for them."

Dowie said, "All right, just let them into my room one at a time and I will talk to them." Two hundred people passed through his room and he didn't pray for one of them. He sent them out without prayer or without

20

ministering to them because he knew they weren't ready.

The two hundred and first one to come was a dear old crippled lady. She was not financially able to buy crutches, so she hobbled along on some sticks. Her limbs were swollen. She had no shoes on, nor could she have worn them, for her feet were swollen and burst open. She had wrapped burlap sacks around her feet. But she went into the room sick and came out perfectly healed and walking normally because Dowie perceived that she had the faith to be healed. She was the only one he laid hands on and prayed for out of several hundred. He had 100 per cent success because the only one he prayed for got healed.

On many occasions as I have taught, I have perceived that someone had faith and I said, "You are ready, come on and get your healing." And when I do it that way, I have 100 per cent success. This is so much better than when we try to minister in a wholesale manner and see just a few healed.

I often tell people, "If you will just give me the same chance you would the doctor, I will get you healed. And it won't cost you a dime." Folks will go to the doctor and if he says, "Come back next Tuesday," they will go back next Tuesday. Then when he says, "Come again Friday," they return on Friday. This may go on for months. However, if I say, "Come back," they get angry.

"Well, I'm not going back anymore. I thought surely he would pray for me," they say. But they may not be ready yet.

Many times a doctor will tell a person, "I am going to put you in the hospital for several days to build you up for an operation." But if I tell them, "I want you to stay in the services for several days to get built up for the operation God is going to perform," they get angry. If they will stay under the sound of the Word of God, it will have an effect upon them. Then the Spirit of God who operates in my life will show me what to do and just how to help that person.

I laid hands on a man facing major surgery. He didn't receive healing. He kept coming back to the meetings, and one night he told me, "I was in that healing line and didn't receive healing. But since you have taught I can see where I missed it. I didn't try to believe anything; I didn't try to receive anything. I just thought if you had it, it would work. I thought if you had it, you would give it to me. Now I see I have my part to play. I am supposed to go to the hospital Friday morning. They want to keep me there several days to build me up for this operation. But I am not going. I'll be back here Friday night in that healing service."

He didn't ask me to pray for him then, or the next night. He said, "I'll be back Friday night in that special laying-on-of-hands service."

Friday night he was the first one in the line. I said, "Well, I see you are here."

"Yes," he said, "I am here. I'll receive my healing, too. Just put your hands on me." He did receive instant healing, and never had to have that operation. I heard from his pastor several years later, and he was still healed.

I have seen people filled with the Holy Spirit in the same way. They have come to be filled with the Spirit, but when I laid hands on them, they didn't receive. Nevertheless, they kept coming back to the services, and as their faith was built up by listening to the Word taught, they did receive.

Many times I tell folks to look at their watch when hands are laid on them, and whether there is a physical manifestation or not, believe they receive then. I have seen people with terminal cancer and other extreme cases healed that way. There wasn't any manifestation at the moment, but they simply looked at their watch and said, "That's it. Praise God, I accept it now." Then the manifestation came.

Why doesn't the manifestation always come instantly?

There are a variety of reasons. One is that healing is by degree, based on two conditions. First, the degree of healing virtue ministered. Second, the degree of the individual's faith that gives action to that healing virtue. If there is no faith to give action to it, it will not be manifested at all, even though the healing virtue is actually ministered.

Many people have said, "When you laid hands on me, I felt the power of God go through me like a bolt of electricity. I felt all right for two or three days, but now every symptom has come back on me." There was no faith on the part of the individual to give action to that power. They knew it was there; they felt God's healing power go into them. But they didn't act on the Word of God.

Before I received my healing a number of years ago, I was bedfast with two serious organic heart troubles and my body was partially paralyzed. As a member of a denominational church, I thought the Bible was true, but I knew nothing about the power of God in operation in healing or miracles. But when I said with my mouth because I believed it in my heart, "I believe I receive my healing...I believe I receive healing for my heart...I believe I receive healing for my paralyzed body," I felt something like a warm glow come down over my head, spread out over my shoulders, down my body, and out the end of my toes. With this my paralysis left and has never been back.

How many more have testified that they felt a warmth that was God's healing power. The testimony of an attorney from a denominational church in Texas describes how he felt something come down over him like a warm glow. It was as if his whole body was bathed in warm oil, he said. He had never come in contact with anything like that before, and it scared him at first. Then he realized that this must be God, and he began to yield to this power.

It seemed that this power lifted him out of bed and put him on the floor. "I stood up and every symptom of my disease left," he said. He went back to the doctors, who, incidentally, had given him up to die. They made X-rays and ran tests, but couldn't find a thing wrong. That was God's healing power. He was by himself—no one laid hands on him. I was in my bedroom by myself—no one laid hands on me. But that same power was manifested.

Everyone who has been baptized in the Holy Ghost has an anointing of the Spirit in them. I John 2:27 says, *"But the anointing which ye have received of him abideth in you...."* You have the right to lay hands in faith on anyone, if they release their faith, and expect them to be healed.

The laying on of hands can also be practiced from the standpoint of the law of transmission. By laying on of hands, one transmits God's healing power unto those sick persons, because he is anointed with that power. Notice that this power does not work automatically. You cannot transfer that healing power to whomever you will. Jesus could not (Mark 6:5).

When the woman with the issue of blood touched Jesus and He felt this power go out of Him He said, *"...who touched my clothes? And his disciples said unto him, Thou seest the multitude thronging thee, and sayest thou, Who touched me?"* There was no way of telling how many people had touched Him just to see if anything would happen. No power flowed out into any of them. *"...he looked round about to see her that had done this thing. But the woman fearing and trembling, knowing what was done in her, came and fell down before him, and told him all the truth. And he said unto her, Daughter, thy faith hath made thee whole...."* (Mark 5:24-34).

Someone said, "I thought it was that healing power that flowed out of Him." Jesus said her faith did it. It was a combination of the two—her faith activated that heal-

24

ing power. It was there all the time, but those other people who touched Him received nothing because there was no faith.

We need to realize that this power is passive and inactive until faith is exercised. It will not operate on its own. As far as we know, that woman was the only one in that whole crowd—and there was a multitude—who was healed. But because she reached out in faith and touched the hem of His garment, she was made whole.

CHAPTER IV

Our Healing—An Accomplished Fact

When screeching air raid sirens signaled another bombing raid in London, England, during World War II, everyone ran to the nearest air raid shelter. Everyone, that is, except one little old lady. The people in her neighborhood were busy during the daytime cleaning up the debris and trying to repair the damage caused by the bombs. Then at night they would huddle for protection in the air raid shelters.

After several nights, some commented that this certain woman was missing. Some speculated that she had been injured and was in the hospital. Someone else mentioned that perhaps she had been killed. Still others thought that she had gone away to the country to escape the bombs. A few days later someone met her on the street during the daytime and said, "Well, we are certainly glad to see you back, and to know that you are all right."

"Oh, I haven't been anywhere," she answered.

"But every night the air raid siren sounds, and the bombs are falling, but you haven't joined us in the air raid shelter. Where have you been?" he asked.

"I was at home sleeping," was her casual reply.

"Sleeping?" he asked, astonished. "How could you sleep through all this? Aren't you scared?"

"No," she answered. "When I was reading in my Bible the other day, I found where it says that God neither slumbers nor sleeps. So I decided that there was no need for both of us to stay awake."

Likewise, if Jesus has borne our sickness—and Isaiah 53:4 says He has—there is no need for us to bear it, too. Looking up the word translated "borne" in this text, we find that in the original Hebrew it meant to "lift up, to bear away, to convey, or to remove to a distance." Therefore, when the scripture says, "He hath borne our sicknesses," it means that He has borne them away, or removed them to a distance.

The word used is a Levitical word, and is applied to the scapegoat that bore the sins of the people. It is the same Hebrew word used in Leviticus 16:22. *"...the goat shall bear upon him all their iniquities..."* The high priest laid his hands upon this goat, and by faith conferred, or transferred, to that goat the sins and the iniquities of Israel. Then the goat was taken out, *"unto a land not inhabited: and he shall let go the goat in the wilderness."*

Just as that goat bore the sins of Israel, the Word of God teaches that Jesus bore my sins and my sicknesses. Sin and sickness have passed from me to Calvary, and salvation and health have passed from Calvary to me.

In the 4th verse of this redemption chapter (Isaiah 53) we have not only the Hebrew verb for borne, but we also have the Hebrew verb for "carried." *"He hath borne our sicknesses, and carried our pains."* These two verbs in the Hebrew are the same as those used in the 11th and 12th verses regarding His substitutionary bearing of sin. *"He shall bear their iniquities...and he bare the sin of many...."* In the Hebrew, the verbs "hath borne" and "carried" signify "to assume as a heavy burden." They denote actual substitution, that He actually took on Himself the burden of our sin, or our sin nature.

It is equally true that He has borne our sicknesses and carried our pains. These verbs in the Hebrew mean a complete removal. When Jesus bore our sins, our sicknesses, and our pains, He bore them away. He completely removed them.

27

Both of these verbs signify substitution. They mean, "One bearing another's load." That is what Jesus did for us. As my substitute He bore my sins and my sicknesses. That is the reason divine healing belongs to every child of God. There is no need to question God's will in the matter when you know this. If He bore our sicknesses and carried our pains, there is no need for both of us to bear them.

This scriptural truth became reality to a woman who came for prayer in one of my meetings. She had a cancer on her face—a purplish-looking malignant growth. I told her, "Just say, 'According to the Word of God, I am healed. I believe this cancer is healed.' According to the Word, it is healed. Go to bed saying it, get up saying it. Say it sweeping the floor, say it washing the dishes. Say it everytime you think of it. I feel led of the Lord to tell you to do this for ten days."

On the tenth day the phone rang in the parsonage. On the other end of the line was this lady who, although nearly too excited to talk, managed to say, "The cancerous growth just came out of my face. It has a lot of roots on it. It all came out, and there is no hole in my face. It is as smooth as a baby's skin."

When was this woman healed? On the tenth day? No, she was healed back there at Calvary, but it was manifested when she believed it. It came about as she said, "According to the Word I am healed." It came about as she believed that Christ, as her substitute, had already borne her sickness, He had paid the price for her cancer, and therefore, she didn't have to bear it any longer.

CHAPTER V

Possessing the Promise

When I tell people that they don't have to pray in order to be healed, they look at me in amazement. But many have failed to receive healing because they have based their faith on prayer instead of on God's Word. They expected prayer to do for them what God's Word will do for them. Praying is only successful when it is based upon the promises in God's Word.

We needn't pray, "God, heal this man; heal this woman." In the mind of God, He has already healed them. Sometimes we pray, "God, save this man." "God, save my son." "God, save that woman." Nowhere does the New Testament say anything about praying for the lost that they will be saved. Jesus said, *"...pray ye therefore the Lord of the harvest, that he would send forth labourers into his harvest"* (Luke 10:2). If you want to pray for someone who is lost, say, "Lord, send someone to minister to them." They can't be saved without it.

When folks come to the altar for prayer, find out what their need is. If a man came to be saved, you could pray for him for six weeks, but unless he acts on what God said, he will get up and go home unsaved. Turn to God's Word. Show him what the Bible says. Get him to act upon it and believe that Word. As far as God is concerned, the man is already saved. From God's standpoint, salvation is already bought and paid for. It is not a matter of God's saving him; it is a matter of his accepting the salvation God offers.

29

It is not a matter of God's baptizing someone with the Holy Ghost. It is a matter of his accepting the gift of the Holy Ghost that God offers. By the same token, it is not a matter of God's healing an individual; it is a matter of his accepting the gift God has already provided.

Someone said, "Well, I believe God is going to heal me sometime. I believe that in His own good time and in His own way He will do it." But that kind of thinking is out of line with the Word. I Peter 2:24 says, *"...by whose stripes ye were healed."* Notice that it says "were," not "going to be." If I believe what the Bible says, then I believe that we *were* healed. Peter is looking back to Calvary. I was healed then. I accept that.

God laid on Him our sicknesses and diseases; He bore them, He was "stricken, smitten of God, and afflicted" with your diseases. Therefore, Satan has no right to put on you what God put on Jesus. Someone may say, "It may be the will of God for me to be sick. God may get more glory out of my being sick than if I were well." What right, then, would God have to put your sickness on Jesus if He wanted you to keep bearing it? There is no need for both of you to bear it. Because He bore it, you are free!

All of God's blessings and provisions are conditional. He gives us His Word to let us know what conditions must be met in order for us to receive these blessings. They won't just fall on us automatically like ripe cherries off a tree. There is a God-ward side and a man-ward side to every battle and to every blessing. God has His part to play, but man has his part to play also.

Paul wrote concerning Israel that what happened to them happened as examples to us, and what was written beforehand was written for our admonition (I Corinthians 10:11). When God led the children of Israel out of Egypt (which is a type of the world), He didn't just deposit them in the wilderness and leave them there. He had a further blessing for them. He not only brought them out of Egypt; He also had another land for them to go into—Canaan's land.

Canaan is a type of the baptism of the Holy Ghost and of our rights and privileges in Christ, which include healing. God had said to the children of Israel again and again that He was going to give them that land. When they finally crossed over the Jordan River into Canaan, God said, *"Every place that the sole of your foot shall tread upon, that have I given unto you, as I said unto Moses"* (Joshua 1:3). God had said He would give them the land, but the people had to possess it.

That's how it is with our rights and privileges in Christ. Healing belongs to us. God has provided it for us. But we have to possess it. Unless we possess the provision, we will not enjoy its benefits.

Many people are just waiting for God to do something about their sickness. "If God ever heals me, then I'm going to believe it." I have talked to sinners who had that same idea about salvation—they left it all up to God. One man said, "If God wants to save me, He will." However, God's Word says that it is His will to save him. God invited him to come. *"...And whosoever will, let him take the water of life freely"* (Revelation 22:17). But the man put all responsibility on God. "When God gets ready, then He will do it. I am just waiting on God." But he died without God.

The believer sometimes makes that same mistake of thinking, "If God wants me to have this, He will give it to me. If I don't get it, then He just doesn't want me to have it." We need to get into the Word of God and find out what belongs to us. If it is promised to us, or if it is provided for us in His Word, then it is His will. All we have to do is to possess it.

We need to settle this because as long as we waver, we will not receive anything. James 1:6-7, says, *"But let him ask in faith, nothing wavering. For he that wavereth is like a wave of the sea driven with the wind and tossed. For let not*

that man think that he shall receive any thing of the Lord."
Often we don't receive because we waver.

Like salvation, healing is a gift, already paid for at Calvary. All we need to do is accept it. All we need to do is possess the promise that is ours. As children of God, we need to realize that *healing belongs to us.*